SPIRIT-CENTERED
RELATIONSHIPS

ALSO BY KATHLYN AND GAY HENDRICKS

CONSCIOUS LOVING: The Journey to Co-Commitment

THE CONSCIOUS HEART: Seven Soul-Choices That Inspire Creative Partnership

LASTING LOVE: The 5 Secrets of Growing a Vital, Conscious Relationship

*ATTRACTING GENUINE LOVE: A Step-by-Step Program to
Bring a Loving and Desirable Partner into Your Life*

❀ ❀ ❀

ALSO BY GAY HENDRICKS

CONSCIOUS LIVING: Finding Joy in the Real World

*THE CORPORATE MYSTIC: A Guidebook for Visionaries
with Their Feet on the Ground*, by Gay Hendricks and Kate Ludeman, Ph.D.

*SPIRITUAL CINEMA: A Guide to Movies That Inspire, Heal, and Empower
Your Life*, by Stephen Simon and Gay Hendricks*

THE BOOK OF LIFE: The Master-Key to Inner Peace and Relationship Harmony.
Epictetus's Handbook of Conscious Living, edited and interpreted
for a new millennium by Gay Hendricks and Philip Johncock*

*THE POWER OF A SINGLE THOUGHT: How to Initiate Major Life Changes from
the Quiet of Your Mind*, revised and edited by Gay Hendricks and Debbie Devoe*

❀ ❀ ❀

All of the above are available at your local bookstore, and the
titles with asterisks (*) may be ordered by visiting:

Hay House USA: **www.hayhouse.com**®
Hay House Australia: **www.hayhouse.com.au**
Hay House UK: **www.hayhouse.co.uk**
Hay House South Africa: **orders@psdprom.co.za**
Hay House India: **www.hayhouseindia.com**

❀ ❀ ❀

SPIRIT-CENTERED RELATIONSHIPS

Gay and Kathlyn Hendricks

HAY HOUSE, INC.
Carlsbad, California
London • Sydney • Johannesburg
Vancouver • Hong Kong

Published and distributed in the United States by: Hay House, Inc.: www.hayhouse. com • *Published and distributed in Australia by:* Hay House Australia Pty. Ltd.: www. hayhouse.com.au • *Published and distributed in the United Kingdom by:* Hay House UK, Ltd.: www.hayhouse.co.uk • *Published and distributed in the Republic of South Africa by:* Hay House SA (Pty), Ltd.: orders@psdprom.co.za • *Distributed in Canada by:* Raincoast: www.raincoast.com • *Published in India by:* Hay House Publications (India) Pvt. Ltd.: www.hayhouseindia.com • *Distributed in India by:* Media Star: booksdivision@ mediastar.co.in

Editorial supervision: Jill Kramer • *Design:* Julie Davison

Library of Congress Control Number: 2005930625

ISBN 13: 978-1-4019-0887-4
ISBN 10: 1-4019-0887-X

09 08 07 06   5 4 3 2
1st printing, January 2006
2nd printing, January 2006

Printed in the United States of America

We dedicate this book to Elsie and Imogen, in gratitude for the love they give us and the wonder they radiate.

CONTENTS

Please note: All of the stories and case studies in this book are true.
All names have been changed for confidentiality purposes.

INTRODUCTION

SPIRIT-CENTERED RELATIONSHIPS:
A NEW PATH TO INTIMACY AND
FULL CREATIVE EXPRESSION

What is a spirit-centered relationship, and how can you bring more genuine love into your life?

To answer these questions, tune in to yourself to find out if this is what your heart desires in a close relationship:

1. You feel connected to your own spiritual essence—your true self—in all the ups and downs of daily living.

2. You and your partner feel connected on the spiritual level, both in times of stress as well as in times of joy and abundance.

3. You grow creatively as independent individuals at the same time that you grow closer together in intimacy.

4. You feel an abundant flow of creative energy because you don't squander it on conflicts that are never resolved.

5. You and your beloved learn to love so generously and wisely that your relationship becomes a sacred treasure to you and an inspiration to others.

If this is the kind of relationship your heart desires, then we believe that you'll find this book liberating, practical, and soul-satisfying.

We set out to create a spirit-centered relationship for ourselves more than 25 years ago. By using the practices we share with you in this book, we transformed our own relationship from struggle and disappointment to a steady source of inspiration and delight. It took years of conscious attention to create the comfortable flow of love and harmony we now celebrate, but the learning and joy we experienced made the journey exhilarating every step of the way.

We believe that the magic is in the tools and your willingness to use them; to that end, we created the relationship of our dreams out of tiny moments of conscious choice. When we got stuck— and it happened hundreds of times in our early years— we simply went back to the practices we share with you in this book. And they worked, *every single time,* to shift us out of our old programming into a new flow of love and harmony.

It was the power of "Presencing" that made our transformation possible, and since then the passionate purpose of our lives has been to help as many people as we can enjoy that remarkable power in their own relationships.

What Is Presencing?

If you look in a dictionary, you probably won't find the verb *To Presence* or the noun *Presencing.* We coined these terms many years ago because we couldn't find any other words that described exactly what we meant. To us, Presencing is the act of resting your attention on something real that you're experiencing right now. As our skill in Presencing grew, we felt a greater connection with the natural spiritual essence of ourselves and each other. In other words, where Presencing goes, spirit flows and relationship grows.

To understand what Presencing feels like, begin with a few moments of it right now. Tune in and feel a sensation that you're presently experiencing in your body—for example, notice if you're thirsty. Whether you are or aren't, thirst is a sensation (or several sensations) that lets you know how you feel. Is it a dryness in your mouth or the absence of that dryness? Is there some other indication that tells you whether you're thirsty or not? Whatever it is, rest your awareness for a moment on the sensations.

Presencing uses nonjudgmental attention. Don't judge or critique or analyze whether you ought to be thirsty or not . . . just notice the sensations and let your attention rest on them.

This is what we mean by Presencing.

Although this example may seem trivial, you'll soon see how a magnificent mansion of love can be built on its simple foundation. Consider another example: Imagine that you're talking to a therapist about your fear of abandonment, and she asks you to Presence this fear. You scan your mind and body, noticing the "butterflies" in your stomach. The sensation is inarguable (nobody could convince you that you're not feeling it), so you rest your attention on it for a moment. It's real and it's right now.

Contrast Presencing with something that's not in the present, such as hoping. When you hope, you're picturing a better future than the one you're experiencing right now. Your mind might be manufacturing images of a better future, but your body is registering how you feel in this present moment.

When you're fully present, you feel a natural inner sense of spiritual connection along with your other natural body sensations. When you're fully present, you feel the movement of spirit in you just as you feel any other sensation such as joy or thirst. When you're fully present, you don't doubt your spiritual nature, because you feel its presence as surely as you feel the beating of your heart or the movement of your breathing. This clear sense of your authentic spiritual nature is the first gift of Presencing.

The second gift is this: When you're fully present in a relationship, you feel a natural spiritual connection with the other person. When you and a partner are *both* fully present in your relationship, you feel your natural spiritual connection with each other. You feel it in the background of everything you do. Your relationship becomes spirit-centered, and in our personal experience, this is life at its best. We feel blessed to have lived this kind of life for many years now. The purpose of our lives is to savor it, and to share what we know about how to create this special form of magic.

❊ ❊ ❊

We'd like to take a moment here to tell you what we mean when we use phrases such as *spiritual center, spiritual connection,* and *spiritual essence.* You've probably encountered these terms before, but we define them *somatically,* which may be different from the ways other people use them. That is, when we use words like *spirit* or *spiritual,* we're talking about something you can feel in your body.

You see, there's a huge difference between the *concept* of *taking* a shower and the actual somatic experience of *taking* that shower. Even with a vivid imagination, you can cogitate on the concept of a shower for hours and not come out feeling refreshed. Two minutes in the real water, though, and you feel completely different. This example is especially true in the area of spirituality, which people have been known to discuss for years without having an actual bodily experience of it.

We're all for a somatic approach to spiritual growth instead of a conceptual one—and if you work mindfully through the experiential portions of this book, you'll be able to feel exactly what we mean.

The Practical Value of Presencing

We offer this book to you in service of one major practical outcome: to feel more genuine love and spiritual connection in your life *right now*. If this is what you want, we're delighted to give you the distilled essence of our life's work in helping people learn to give and receive love more generously and wisely.

The simple, graceful practices we call Presencing radiate an extraordinary power to bring new dimensions of love into your life. Whether you're currently single or in an intimate relationship, you can create a new flow of love and harmony through Presencing. When you employ these practices, you'll not only feel more love, you'll also deepen the spiritual connection you experience in your close relationships.

We've come to believe that spirituality and relationship go hand in hand with each other, married for all eternity. We are convinced that spiritual growth is crucial to healthy relationships, and we are also certain that healthy relationships are crucial to spiritual development. Without a spiritual foundation, relationships cannot grow to their full expression; and without relationships, there is no place to see the practical results of your spiritual development. If you master the practices of Presencing we teach in this book, you can feel and see remarkable growth in your spiritual connection with friends, lovers, and yourself.

We base our confidence in the power of Presencing on two kinds of experiences. First, we've celebrated a quarter century of love, abundance, and creativity in our own marriage. Presencing illuminated our way every day—we don't believe that we ever could have attained the level of love and harmony we enjoy without that practice. Second, our confidence in Presencing is built on counseling more than 3,500 couples and many thousands of single people. In our seminars and in our counseling office, we've had the rare pleasure of assisting people with every conceivable relationship issue: money, sex, child rearing, divorce, reconciliation, and much more. Based on all this experience, we're more excited than ever about the possibilities for human transformation through the practice of Presencing.

Here's our promise to you: If you'll invest the time in learning how to do just three practices in your relationships, you can create breakthroughs that may seem like miracles. We've seen such miracles thousands of times, yet they never fail to move us.

If you've ever struggled with love and its wild dynamics, you need to know that there is real hope for all of us. So here are the three skills we'd like you to learn:

1. Presencing wonder
2. Presencing spirit
3. Spirit-centered listening

Each one of these has the power to elevate you to a new level of love and harmony, but when they're practiced together, the results are nothing short of miraculous. All three are actions you take, not beliefs you must adopt or concepts you need to remember. Later in the book you'll find out how to practice them (along with instructions on how to use the enclosed CD, which further illustrates these techniques). For now, though, we'll give you a brief introduction to them so that you'll be able to get a conceptual handle on what they are.

1. Presencing wonder is the first key to creating a thriving spirit-centered relationship. This act will transport you out of your current thinking about relationships into a state of genuine wonder. It will help you break free of habitual patterns and problems, creating an openness to new possibilities. Whether you wish to attract new love into your life or feel more love in a long-standing partnership, in this book you'll discover how you can work real miracles simply through moments of genuine wonder.

2. Presencing spirit is the second action that creates a spirit-centered relationship. It's learning to rest your present-moment awareness on inner experiences (such as feelings) without interrupting, judging, or analyzing them. When you can do this, you'll invite forth the natural spiritual feeling that's in the background of your inner experience all the time. It takes practice for most people to learn how to notice this feeling because attention tends to be diverted by the noisier sensations of hunger, anxiety, and sexual attraction. We were surprised and delighted to discover, however—both in ourselves and with our clients—that natural sensations of spiritual connection are always there, waiting to be invited into the foreground.

"Presencing spirit" is the name we gave to this process, because when you learn to do it well, you'll feel an unmistakable sense of deeper spiritual connection inside you. As you master this practice, you'll feel a greater sense of internal space and freedom. You'll give your inner experience, especially your feelings, room to breathe—that is, you're literally letting them be. A clear awareness of increasing your inner space is the practical sensory feeling that lets you know that you're growing spiritually.

3. Spirit-centered listening is the third practice that builds a spirit-centered relationship. As you use this process, you'll create a space in which your partner gets in touch with more dimensions of him- or herself. When you're in this space, you can hear beyond the words to understand the spirit of what your partner is saying.

Once we discovered how to do spirit-centered listening, our own relationship shifted permanently to a much deeper level of harmony. Even now, after teaching it to more than 20,000 people in our seminars, we're still moved by the power of this simple technique to increase the flow of love in close relationships.

How Will _You_ Benefit?

Why do we believe so firmly that you'd benefit from learning the practices of Presencing? To answer that question, take a moment to open the door to your own relationships and have a look around. For example, take a moment to think about the following:

— Have you ever been locked in a struggle about sex or money . . . one that never seemed to get resolved no matter how many times you argued about it? We have, too, and although it's been many years since we last felt the hot frustration of that dilemma, even the memory of it makes us squirm.

— Are you single or divorced? If so, have you ever despaired that you might never draw someone who was really there for you into your life? We've both been there, and we now believe it was the power of Presencing that set us free to find the love of our lives (each other).

— If you're in a committed relationship, have you ever felt a period of strain or distance in it? You tried everything you could think of to break through the impasse, but nothing you did could penetrate the wall. We can certainly relate to this as well.

These have been some of the most difficult things we've personally ever had to endure. In fact, compared to the relentless numbing anguish of relationship conflict, the sharp pain of a broken limb or a cut almost feels luxurious. When you have a physical injury, you can sense that it will have a middle and an end—with relationship pain, however, you're never quite sure that it's *ever* going to be over.

Both of us had experienced our share of relationship pain by the time we met each other in our early 30s, so we were highly committed to finding a better way. Here's the surprising discovery we made, first in our own marriage and later in many counseling sessions: Almost all relationship problems, even the most painful ones, are wake-up calls to *be present* to something. In other words, when you finally pause long enough to be present to a problem, that very act begins to dissolve it.

We believe that the reason for this phenomenon is explained by a concept attributed to Albert Einstein: You cannot *solve* a problem in the same state of consciousness in which it was *created*. We state this concept positively: The only way to solve a problem is to get out of the state of consciousness that created it and into one that allows it to resolve.

Presencing has that power—which comes from its reliable ability to take any of us rapidly into a new state of consciousness. A few moments of Presencing and everything changes! Often it works so fast that you can hardly believe it. It's real, though, and best of all, the new state of consciousness feels intrinsically good. It's a euphoric feeling that comes not from a drug but from your own natural resources.

Presencing Is a New Meta-Method

Now if you've struggled with big challenges in your relationships, you need more than a set of new techniques to help you—you need a "meta-method" (or a new, transcendent method) that takes you above and beyond the realm in which problems occur. The good news is that a meta-method actually exists, and it really works. The even better news is that it's not hard to learn—if you can drive a car, multiply four times four, or even operate a toaster, you have more than enough mental ability to learn Presencing. The rest is done with heart, soul, and practice.

We've seen Presencing restore passion to long-dead relationships, and we've seen it bring the miracle of new love to single people who'd given up. If you invest a few hours in learning Presencing, you'll gain an immense power in the most important area of your life. Love will always be a mystery, but as you learn Presencing, it will start to be about mastery.

Speaking Personally

We feel incredibly blessed to have enjoyed 25 years of a rich, joyful relationship with each other. Along the way we've savored other joys of life, such as raising successful kids and creating financial abundance, but the foundation of it all is the flow of love and harmony between us. When it comes right down to it, feeling the flow of love and harmony is probably the most important thing in life. If you don't feel it, you're probably not going to be truly happy, no matter how much money you have or how well your kids are doing.

As the philosopher Tasso said, "Any time not spent on love is wasted." So let's not waste a moment! After all, your time is precious, and they're not making as much of it as they used to. Turn the page and begin your journey toward a new world of love and harmony.

❀ ❀ ❀ ❀

PART I

THE THREE KEYS TO
A SPIRIT-CENTERED
RELATIONSHIP

CHAPTER ONE

PRESENCING WONDER:
YOUR FIRST STEP IN CREATING A
SPIRIT-CENTERED RELATIONSHIP

Great journeys begin in wonder, so if you want to make big changes in your relationship life, begin with a brief moment of it. Even a split second of genuine wonder breaks you free from the prison of your old thinking, opening a zone of creative possibility within you. The practice we call "Presencing wonder" gives you a clear space from which you can launch a new life.

Right here, right now, we'd like you to pause to circulate some of the biggest "wonder-questions" of all through your heart and mind: "Am I willing to feel loved and loving all the time? And could I let love be easy for me—always and in all ways?" This little experiment will give you a chance to notice what wonder actually feels like in your body and mind.

Think about your love life as it exists right now. You might be single or in a partnership, or you might be in transition from one to the other—but wherever you are, you probably have worries about it. Focus in on one of those concerns right now: Pick one that you've thought about a lot and that hasn't

seemed to change in a positive direction, but would make a big difference to you if it did. For example, suppose you've been single for a while and you worry that you might not ever find a love relationship that's right for you. Or suppose you've been in a long-term partnership and you're afraid that some aspect of it (such as sex, money, or parenting) is never going to change. Be sure to pick one that matters.

Now let's put the power of wonder to the test. Take a moment to invoke it, and then notice how it changes your whole being in a positive direction. Later, notice how such a simple practice brings about a positive change in the actual circumstances of the issue.

Here's how to do it. First, phrase your concern in a simple sentence, such as "I fear that I'm never going to find a love that's right for me," or "I'm worried that my partner and I are never going to stop fighting about money."

Next, take the very same concern . . . and wonder about it instead of worrying. Change it into a wonder-question, such as "I wonder how I can go about finding a lover who's just right for me," or "I wonder how my partner and I can generate financial abundance." If you do this sincerely, you'll actually be able to feel the despair melt from your body. You'll notice that the unpleasant sensations dissolve and are replaced by the fresh, positive feeling of wonder.

Now, try on a deeper experience. Look back over your entire relationship journey up until this very moment. Think of your first love(s), and recall the joys of discovering it—as well as the heartbreak, betrayals, or rejections you may have experienced. Reflect on all the significant love relationships of your life, calling to mind their ups and downs and highs and lows. When you've brought all that to mind, treat yourself to a moment of genuine wonder by asking yourself this: "What would my life be like if all of that had happened in some other way?"

Did you experience an open space in your mind right after you asked this question? That's what happens when you practice Presencing wonder—which has an awesome power to create a different and better future for you in the most important part of your life.

Couples Who Wonder

Now let's shift gears to the story of a lifesaving change that began in a few seconds of genuine wonder. Through a spontaneous moment of Presencing, two people were able to break free from a downward spiral of addiction that seemed certain to continue until they both wound up dead.

Sasha and Alec were both alcoholics even before they met, and their marriage became a ten-year cycle of long, drunken binges followed by periods of remorse and recovery. Along the way they squandered a trust fund, lost their home and cars, trashed their once-promising careers, and nearly died on several occasions.

At the bottom of the spiral, they awoke from a two-week bender/blackout. By grace or just some darn good luck, they somehow managed to generate a moment of genuine wonder when she turned to him and said, "I wonder if we can find a better way."

He replied, "I don't know. What if it's too late?"

Sasha asked, "But what if it isn't? When I woke up I found myself wondering if we could do it all a different way, without the booze or drugs. Do you want to try?"

Alec thought about it for a moment and said, "Yes."

From this quiet moment of wonder, the couple was able to birth a new life. Within three years they'd built new careers, bought a house, and created a supportive circle of friends. In fact, when we met them, they were both sober and engaged in community services of various kinds. A once-unimaginable life now seemed normal to them. In telling their story at one of our seminars, they highlighted the decidedly undramatic nature of their moment of wonder. Although it wasn't accompanied by thunderclaps or bolts of lightning, one taste of genuine wonder got them off the treadmill to oblivion they were stuck on. That moment set them forth on a new life journey.

In fact, moments of Presencing wonder are often just like that: quiet and simple. The only thing that matters is that they're sincere. You can't fake it—after all, everyone knows what wonder feels like because we've all been children. Most of us also know the pain of leaving wonder behind—we know what it feels like to trade it in for the structures of certainty that adult life is built upon, and we all know how drab and flat that wonder-less life of certainty can be. That's why Presencing feels so refreshing and creates change so rapidly: One moment of it and we're back in childhood, where dreams are born and possibilities are infinite.

Now you may not have quite as much baggage to let go of as Sasha and Alec, but it's nice to know that wonder can work its magic even in desperate circumstances. And practically speaking, we've found that people never resolve any relationship problem unless they're willing to suspend their habitual viewpoint in favor of a moment of genuine wonder.

To clearly understand what we mean, listen to this bit of dialogue from the first session one of us had with Jim and Jan, a couple who came to discuss a sexual problem of long duration (note that nonverbal cues, along with our commentary, are bracketed and in italics).

Kathlyn: Would you be willing to create a thriving sexual relationship with each other?

Jim: We've never really had anything like that, not even in the beginning. *[Notice that he immediately disregards Kathlyn's invitation to be willing now, and responds from the perspective of how it's always been in the past.]*

Jan: He doesn't believe in things like foreplay.

Jim: Aw, that's totally unfair.

Kathlyn: I can feel how much anger and hurt you both have about this subject. I'm glad you're willing to bring those feelings out and give them some breathing room. Take a few breaths and acknowledge all the anger and sadness you feel about all of this. *[They pause for a few moments and shift their attention to taking some deep breaths.]* Good. Now would you be willing to make another shift? *[They nod yes.]* Right now, check inside yourselves and find out if you're willing to solve the problem.

Jim: How do we do that?

Jan: Yeah, how?

Kathlyn: The first step is being willing—then maybe we can find out how. But I know from past experience that nothing will happen unless you're willing for it to happen now. *[The couple looks at each other for a moment.]* Let me ask you my original question again: Would you be willing to create a thriving sexual relationship with each other?

Jan and Jim: Yes.

Kathlyn: Okay, great. Now let's take a moment to wonder together how we can make that happen as soon as possible. Have you ever wondered about something that you really didn't know the answer to? *[Now that they've established their willingness, Kathlyn begins a process of inviting them to experience a few moments of Presencing wonder.]*

Jan: Like whether there's an afterlife? Or thinking about what you're going to do when you grow up?

Kathlyn: Those are good examples. You really wondered about them, and you didn't know the answer.

Jim: Yeah. Or like wondering if you were going to get into a college you wanted to get into?

Kathlyn: Yes. So take a moment right now to think about how you can create a great sex life with each other. Put aside everything that's happened in the past, and channel all your energy into wondering what's possible now. *[They sit for about 30 seconds, with rapt expressions of curiosity and attention on their faces.]*

Jan: There's sort of a freedom in that, isn't there?

Kathlyn: Yes. Tell me some more about what you're feeling.

Jan: Well, it feels very good and open inside—not really knowing, but open to knowing.

Jim: I slip in and out of it. I'll have a second of really wondering, then I'll have a memory of something that happened in the past.

Kathlyn: Yes, that's very natural. Our minds aren't used to wondering much once we "grow up." We need to practice to remember how to do it again.

Many of us, especially if we've been wounded in our close relationships, carry within us a reservoir of despair and bitterness. If you're standing in the middle of that reservoir, it makes it hard to visualize a life that's not flavored by the bitterness. That's why genuine wonder—even a moment of it—is so important. It lifts you free of the experiences of the past and creates a clearing inside you.

Remember Einstein's concept: You can't solve a problem in the same state of consciousness that created it. Wonder lifts you into a new state of consciousness, one that you can clearly feel in your own mind and body.

Putting Wonder to Work in Your Life Right Now

As you move along through the concepts and practices in this book, pause often to really wonder about how you can open yourself up more to the flow of love and spiritual connection that's always available around and within you. Love and spiritual connection are your natural states, your birthright. And the good news—the literally wonder-full news—is that this nurturing wellspring of inner delight is brought to full flow by a natural power that you already have in abundance.

❀ ❀ ❀ ❀

CHAPTER TWO

PRESENCING SPIRIT:

HOW TO FEEL YOUR SPIRITUAL CENTER

IN EVERY RELATIONSHIP MOMENT

In this chapter, you'll be working with the second key to building a spiritual relationship: "Presencing spirit." There are two main benefits to practicing this skill. First, you'll learn how to feel your organic spiritual nature as a bodily experience, not as a concept you have to think about. With practice, you can feel your spiritual essence as easily as you can feel the warmth of the sun on your skin. This ability makes it much easier to enjoy the second benefit: seeing the spiritual nature of people you're close to. When you feel your own spiritual essence—and can also see the divinity at the core of your partner—you can move through relationship challenges more quickly and spend more time in the sweet spot of love and harmony.

The feeling of your spiritual essence occurs at a much deeper level than opinions about spirituality. That is, you can have completely different beliefs from your partner about spirituality, but if you both can feel your spiritual essence, you'll have a deep connection that will allow you to be close in spite of big differences on the surface.

Through lots of trial and error in teaching 20,000 people how to enjoy these benefits, we've refined a sequence of learning experiences that can help you acquire the skills rapidly. We invite you to go through these steps carefully, in the sequence we offer them, so you can immediately enjoy the benefits for yourself.

Here is the sequence: First, learn how to be present with your own inner experience, including your natural feelings such as sadness, joy, anger, and fear. Second, learn how to be fully present with others while they're experiencing all *their* natural feelings. A key aspect of learning both these skills is to rest your present-centered awareness on feelings—yours and others'—without attempting to control them or make them better. As you get better at doing these two things, you'll spontaneously begin to incorporate the special practice we call Presencing spirit.

If you learn to be present with your natural feelings and those of others, you'll discover a remarkable fact of life and love: All your feelings—even the unpleasant-seeming ones like anger, sadness, and fear—can put you directly in touch with your spiritual essence. When you learn to be with your emotions in the way we'll show you in this chapter, you can feel any emotion, pleasant or unpleasant, while at the same time being in contact with the sweet sensation of your spiritual essence. It's quite magical to experience, but it's also the kind of magic that you can teach yourself to do every day.

Feel What We Mean Right Now

This practice hinges on learning to be in the present moment. Everything is available in the present, and nothing is available at any other time. So if you're in the present, you can get all the love you want and need; if you're not in the present, you're in a place where your needs can never be met. The past is gone and beyond your control, and the future isn't here yet. It doesn't matter whether the script of your past is a tragedy or a comedy, whether you won or whether you lost—all that matters is that you open a space of possibility *right now* that the love you desire is available in this present moment.

Take a moment to treat yourself to a whole-brain, whole-body example of what we mean. Tune in to something you're feeling right now: It can be something very simple, such as an itch, a quivering sensation, a warmth in your chest, or a pleasant or unpleasant taste in your mouth. Whatever you pick, let your attention rest on it. Just feel it—definitely don't try to understand it just yet. Right now, simply rest your awareness on it.

When you've finished doing that for a moment, read on.

Presencing Your Own Natural Feelings

You can use Presencing spirit with many things, but in order for your relationships to work well, there's one thing you really need to use it with first: your feelings. Emotions are some of the sacred territories of close relationships, well worth many pilgrimages across their holy grounds. And as they're mostly made up of body sensations, it's easiest to begin there. For example, if you're feeling anxious or scared, the main way you know it is by the information from your bodily sensations. You may feel speedy or antsy or have butterflies in your belly, which tells you that you're scared. If you're sensing a heart-heavy pressure in your chest and a lump in your throat, that might indicate that you're sad.

In learning to be present with your feelings, it doesn't matter which ones you focus on. It could be tiredness, hunger, sadness, or happiness; it could even be something sharp like a toothache or a cramp—the important thing is to learn how to rest your attention on the sensations and leave your attention on them *without judging or trying to fix them.*

This simple thing is so important because if you can't do it, you're going to feel out of touch and out of balance inside yourself, as well as with your partner. It's also crucial because almost every relationship conflict is caused by one person (or both people) trying to avoid dealing with something in the present that needs to be acknowledged.

Here's an example of what we mean. Fifty-year-old Carla came to see us a few years ago, explaining that she was feeling depressed because her husband had left her six months before. She also told us that she'd been prescribed three different kinds of antidepressants, but she hadn't liked the side effects of any of them. So, during the first session, we taught her the practice you'll be learning shortly, for we wanted to make sure that she had a natural way to chase the clouds of depression away. The Presencing-spirit process worked wonders for her mental health, but its real magic didn't become clear until Carla came in the following week. She excitedly told us that she'd had a big insight: The real reason for her depression had spontaneously popped into her mind during one of the daily practice sessions we'd asked her to carry out with the Presencing-spirit process.

We were sitting on the edge of our seats to hear what happened, and we weren't disappointed. Carla said that during her practice session something occurred to her that made her start laughing out loud. She said that she laughed so hard she started sobbing, which then turned back into laughter. You see, she'd remembered wondering—a year before her husband left— if there was any way she could get out of her marriage because she'd felt so stifled, trapped, and unfulfilled. She remembered wondering and wishing along these lines for a couple of months, then putting away the idea as unrealistic. With a sheepish look on her face, Carla told us that she'd also had a number of fantasies of what it would be like if her husband died suddenly.

A year after submerging this midlife desire for freedom, our client got her liberation handed to her by her husband's departure. With wonder on her face as she told us this story, she said, "I even started the big fight that led to his leaving that night." Then she added, "I got so caught up in the drama of being left by my husband that I didn't realize until this week that I'd wished for the whole thing a year before."

Quite understandably, Carla's family had originally rushed to her rescue by casting her in the role of victim, while her soon-to-be-ex was banished from the clan's gatherings, frozen in the role of perpetrator. The net effect of this drama was a major bout of depression for our client—but fortunately she found her way back to her usual high-energy state by diligently ending the drama.

Carla told her family members (including her husband) about the insight she'd shared with us, and gently requested that if they really loved her, they'd stop thinking of her as a victim. She ended up quitting her job as a medical receptionist and going back to finish the college degree she'd put aside 20-some years ago. Last we heard from her she was in a graduate program, on her way to becoming an accountant.

Carla's story illustrates that if a significant feeling occurs inside you and you don't know how to be present with it, you'll lose contact with something essential that's very likely worth your attention. It's like driving a car: If you hear a rattle in the engine and don't pay attention to it (perhaps turning up the radio to drown out the irritating racket), your entire journey could be ruined. And so it goes in relationships.

A Deeper Experiment

Things like itches, aches, and other bodily sensations may not always be significant, but they're great opportunities to practice Presencing. They're unmistakable and unarguable, so if you can learn to be present with them, you'll be better able to do the same with the more complicated feelings of anger, fear, sadness, and joy.

So right now, give yourself the gift of a deeper experiment in learning how to be present with your feelings. See if you feel any of the following in your body right now:

- The heavy lump-in-the-throat sensation of sadness
- The antsy-butterfly sensation of fear
- The tight-jaw, tight-neck sensation of anger
- The warm, openhearteded sensation of love and joy

Choose one and rest your attention on it. We say "rest" because we'd like this to be easygoing and playful rather than an effort, so let your attention land as gently as a butterfly might alight on a leaf.

Now, as you rest your attention on the sensation you've chosen, let go of any urge to fix it or make it better . . . simply let it be. Open your heart to the sensation and embrace it with pure acceptance. It's rare in life to simply *be* with something instead of trying to improve or get rid of it. Savor that rare treasure right now, resting your awareness on it with no other agenda than to be with it.

Here's why this is such a key first step: Your feelings of natural divinity are always present, but they're usually overshadowed by the more attention-getting sensations of hunger, anger, fear, and the like. When you learn to be with your feelings in a nonjudgmental way, you automatically open up a natural connection with your spiritual essence. The reason is that the same internal attitude of "letting things be" is the same one that opens the connection with spirit.

Notice what happens when you get your attention fully connected with the sensation. How long does your attention stay on it? What does your attention jump to when it slips off onto something else? There are no right answers—simply notice what you notice.

Presencing Invites Major Life Change

Ken Hecht, a television producer and writer in Los Angeles, is one of those rare people who lost a great deal of weight (more than 120 pounds) and has kept it off for many years. And a remarkable moment of Presencing changed his life direction. He wrote of the experience in *Newsweek* magazine and has given us permission to share it with you.

In Ken's own words:

How does a person summon the strength to lose the weight? The brutal part is the anxiety-ridden moments leading up to the eating binge. Those moments when it's all internalized and it all seems to be about food. You know you want the food, lots of it, but you know you shouldn't eat it; you know the disgust you'll feel for yourself. But you really want the food, and you know that if only for a few moments— those moments you spend eating it—the food will make the anxiety go away. So then you cave in and gobble, gobble, gobble. Then you hate yourself. The cycle never ends.

For me the key to breaking that cycle was to finally decide one night to give in to the anxiety. Not numb it with the food, but instead go, rather than eat, cold turkey. I wanted to just sir there and see if the nightmarish anxiety I so feared would in fact total me. So I sat and felt god-awful and eventually felt feelings of self-loathing and disgust and worthlessness. And finally the panicky desire to eat passed. It lasted less than 30 minutes. It was an awful experience, and one that I highly recommend. Sit with yourself. Don't eat, don't go to a movie, don't turn on the television. Do nothing but sit quietly, be miserable and feel what you're terrified of. It is the part of yourself you've been using food to run from. It is a part of yourself you need to know.

Doing this just once changed my life. No, I didn't immediately and easily diet the weight off from that point forward. There were many binges. But there were also many times when the anxiety came and I drew upon that one experience and knew I could tough it out. And the next morning there's a wonderful feeling: an absence of self-loathing.

What Ken describes so passionately is a moment of Presencing. Eating was a way to avoid being present with his fear. The food fantasies were his unconscious way of saying, "Let's do something (anything!) else to get out of the present." So he dropped the addiction for a half an hour and Presenced his fear. His advice to others: "Have this one experience that lets you know you can survive what you dread. It will change your life."

It's Human Nature to Avoid Presencing

Most of us find lots of ways *not* to be present—in fact, there's a learned human tendency to avoid Presencing altogether. Ken Hecht avoided his fear by eating, finally waking up 128 pounds into this bad dream, while other people avoid dealing with their issues through substance abuse or even by watching too much

TV. There are hundreds of different ways to avoid, but only one way to become present.

Mary, a former client of ours, told us about an experience of Presencing that changed her life. She was sitting at home alone on a Friday night, when images of a co-worker to whom she was attracted kept popping into her head. She knew from other colleagues that he'd been separated from his wife for a while, and Mary thought that she'd been picking up some indications that he was attracted to her. It occurred to her to Presence her feelings; when she did, she found that she was both excited and scared. Then it was almost as if she went into a trance.

Mary raided the refrigerator looking for something to eat. Finding nothing that appealed to her, she went into her bedroom and cleaned out a closet. Along the way, she tried on clothes and set out some shoes for polishing. Then she "woke up" and realized that she was avoiding Presencing her fear and excitement. She went back and sat down in the chair where it had all started, and she let herself tune in to her sensations of fear and excitement and sit with them until they passed. Suddenly, it occurred to her to call the co-worker at home— an idea that brought up another wave of fear and excitement, which she Presenced. Then Mary decided to risk it and reached for the telephone.

The co-worker seemed surprised but happy that she'd called. Instead of making small talk, Mary basically summarized the experiences she'd been through over the past hour or so. Her candor inspired him to tell her about his feelings of attraction to her—and they ended up meeting at a nearby coffeehouse.

If you remember how your feelings tended to be dealt with as a child, you'll see why as an adult you have little familiarity with being present with your feelings. In one of our seminars we asked the roomful of people to recall what they'd been told as children when they said they were scared. We filled up a chalkboard with their answers, which included: "Don't be scared," "There's nothing to be afraid of," "Big boys/girls don't get scared," and "Go out and play and get your mind off it." Several people also remembered being taught the Boy Scout remedy for fear: When you're scared, smile and whistle.

None of these pieces of advice are bad; it's just that they're all ways of avoiding being present with the fear. And feelings like anger often engender even more repressive reactions than fear on the part of our caretakers.

In contrast, one of Milton Erickson's students remembered watching how the great psychiatrist dealt with his son's pain when the little boy hurt his leg. Dr. Erickson, knowing the value of being present as a healing and pain-reducing strategy, said something like, "It hurts, Robert. It hurts awfully. And you know what? It's going to keep on hurting for a while." One moment of this brilliant and caring communication could set in motion a lifetime of successful handling of feeling. It had an immediate effect on the little boy's pain, too: As he quit resisting it, it lessened. By not trying to get away from the discomfort—by staying with it—he felt the magic of transformation through the power of his own consciousness.

Ask yourself a question: In your life, particularly your young life, did anyone ever ask you to just be with a feeling? Speaking personally, we can't remember a single incident of it. How did Ken Hecht get the idea to just be with his anxiety after a lifetime of using food to stifle it? One thing's for sure: He probably didn't learn it in school or from his family. In Western culture, there isn't much information available on the value of being present with feelings. Think about it: When we turn on the TV, we don't see any commercials for being present. Imagine a kind white-haired doctor/actor saying "Got a headache? Suffer from nagging backache? Don't take a pill—instead, be with that pain. Open up to it, and acknowledge the feelings under it."

❋ ❋ ❋

One barrier to being present is the lack of any meaningful training in how to do it; another is that the power of Presencing generates resistance to itself. As we saw in Ken Hecht's example, a few minutes of being present can spark a major lifestyle change. Most of us are fairly well addicted to the way things are, though, so we often resist experiences that could shake up the status quo. Being present has a great deal of power in it· the power to irrevocably alter the structures and assumptions by which we live. Of course, most of us desperately want to break out of our ruts, but before we can, we need to acknowledge the part of us that's deeply committed to staying stuck.

When you're stuck, one part of your mind is working against another part—that is, the part that wants to change versus the part that doesn't. You see, your mind knows that you've done things the same way for years and *survived,* so to change is to trade in a sure thing for the radical uncertainties of the unknown. Many of us are equipped with various self-sabotage mechanisms, an internal committee of Luddites who trash the machinery when we begin to make progress.

This reminds of us Michael, a Vietnam veteran we worked with to resolve some recurring relationship issues. His wife, Teri, was complaining about his lack of communicativeness—she felt that she had to draw him out or else try to read his mind to find out what was going on with him. Michael was a consummate stonewaller: In the first few sessions with us, his expression was blank, and he imparted little information about himself. Finally, however, he began to open up, as he started to realize the cost of not being with himself and his emotions. He talked about feeling lonely and isolated at work, and he spoke of the pain of being out of touch with his wife.

At one point, Michael gripped his fists tightly and said that he sensed a pressure building up inside him. We asked him to simply let himself be with that pressure, to really exprerience its sensations. He stared straight ahead for a few moments, breathing more and more deeply. Suddenly, his eyes darted to the right and back to center, and he paled slightly.

We asked him, "What happened? What did you see?"

"Dead bodies," he replied, and started to sob.

Being present for a brief moment had given Michael direct access to feelings he'd been holding since the end of the war. Over the next three sessions he let himself consciously feel many different things—fear, anger, sadness—that he'd sealed off when he was in the military. As he softened to allow these emotions to come into his awareness, Teri noticed a striking difference in their relationship. As she put it, "Michael became more easygoing and easy to touch. He'd seek me out to talk about feelings, something I'd wanted him to do for years."

Within a few weeks, Teri and Michael had rebirthed the flow of love and harmony that they thought had been lost for good. And it all began with a moment of Presencing.

The Internal Critic

Another common barrier to being present is the dictatorship of the internal critic, that nagging, harsh voice that tells us we're wrong . . . all the time. The internal critic is by nature a judge, and we've rarely heard it make a favorable judgment; in fact, thousands of our clients have described its paralyzing effect.

Here are some of the commands and criticisms the critic makes:

- "Can't you just sit still and pay attention for a minute?"
- "How many times do I have to tell you?"
- "Has your brain gone out to lunch?"
- "Listen! It's very simple if you'll just pay attention!"
- "You don't seem to have the brains God gave a cow."
- "That was the stupidest thing I've ever seen! What were you thinking of?"

For our client Lewis, the emergence of the critic was always signaled by a fleeting look of disdain. At first he wouldn't speak when the critic was present; instead, he'd just shut down and feel blank. But then he gradually began to bring the critic out into the light of consciousness, telling us, "I just had a critical thought, like *You sure are stupid.*"

Lewis is dyslexic and had a lot of discouraging experiences in school. (Now in his 40s, he attended grade school well before the time when learning disabilities were acknowledged.) His chronic frustration and sense of failure evolved into an internal critic that never seemed to leave him alone.

We had him spend time being present with the internal critic, reclaiming and embracing its need to control. He discovered that the purpose of his inner voice was to protect him from feeling that he was fundamentally flawed and worthless—and little by little, he started to turn his attention to where he felt this fear of "fundamental flawed-ness" in his body. Then he learned to be present with this fear as a bodily sensation. In other words, he learned to feel his fear with no attempt to criticize or judge it.

Lewis described the result of being present in words befitting a poet: "It's a sweet freedom I've never experienced, as if I had a permanent smile in my belly." As if by magic, his internal critic gradually became quiet, and his mind became an oasis of peace instead of a cauldron of self-loathing.

* * *

Karltried Graf Dürckheim, in a hard-to-find book called *Hara,* wrote that "the separation from [a person's] Being is what produces the basic tension in life: the release of it is imperative for the integration of [the] I-self with [the] essence." He believed that the self we learn in order to survive in the world is different from our true essence. In anticipation of the body-centered revolution that would come 50 years later, he localized this learned-for-survival self in the chest, in what is often called fight-or-flight breathing. His theory was that when breathing drops from the chest to the belly, consciousness changes from survival-oriented to essence-centered.

Most people feel that they need to do something immediately when a feeling occurs—they're compelled to get rid of it, control it, or change it into something different. A long time ago, when basic human emotions evolved, they were usually designed to mobilize us for action; now, after several thousand years of civilization, we're learning not to take many of the actions our ancestors were programmed to take. For example, it isn't socially acceptable for us to flee the office or swing a fist when the boss is criticizing us, although that is what our physical machinery might like us to do.

It takes a heroic act of sustained attention to break free of this old programming so that you can feel what you really feel. Ultimately, your ability to be present with the truth in yourself opens up the space for love. The same act of being present to your feelings will eventually amplify the love and spiritual connection you experience—if, that is, you practice patiently and diligently.

Complete instructions for Presencing spirit are given in Part II and on the CD that accompanies this book. We highly recommend that you take the time to go through these instructions carefully so you can feel their full power at work.

Putting Presencing Spirit to Work in Your Life

Daily existence is full of opportunities to lose your spiritual center and then get it back again. Arguments, traffic jams, money squabbles, illness—in Zorba the Greek's memorable words, "the whole catastrophe"—this is what we all contend with in daily life, and it's why Presencing spirit can be such a boon in the experience of living. Every moment of every day brings one opportunity after another to drift away from your spiritual center, then catch the drift and come back home to feel the sweet essence of who you really are.

It's natural and normal to drift, and we suggest that you don't focus on *whether* you drift—rather, measure your progress by how quickly you notice that you've drifted, and how quickly you can return to awareness of your spiritual center. If next month at this time you're catching your drifts faster and returning to your spiritual center sooner, give yourself a bow of appreciation for putting Presencing spirit to work in your life.

❋ ❋ ❋ ❋

CHAPTER THREE

SPIRIT-CENTERED LISTENING:

HOW TO FACILITATE THE FLOW

OF SPIRITUAL CONNECTION

"Spirit-centered listening" occurs when you listen to other people while being aware of your spiritual essence *and* theirs. Another way to say it is that you listen from your spiritual center rather than your ego center. When you practice this technique, you create a space that draws the other person closer to his or her own spiritual center. And when you can practice it with your lover, your communication will become a spiritual practice in itself, continually deepening your connection with yourselves and each other.

Spirit-centered listening varies quite a bit from ego-centered listening and produces very different results; however, it's important to note that neither are right or wrong. It's normal and natural for all of us to slip into ego-centered listening, for reasons that we'll explain in a moment—the problem is when we get stuck in it and don't know how to get out. One of our goals in this book is to show you a liberating alternative when you find yourself locking into ego-centered listening.

A great gift of deeper spiritual awareness in yourself is the ability to find your way back to that awareness when you've lost track of it. As you feel more centered in the sweet sensation of clear spirit inside you, you'll naturally become more adept at finding your way back to that sensation when it gets overshadowed by the shock and awe of daily living.

The word *spirit* is derived from words that mean "breath" in ancient languages. Like your breathing, your spiritual essence is always there nurturing you, even when you're sound asleep. Being in the grip of ego-centered listening, on the other hand, is a little bit like dozing off. When your ego is busily defending you, you're out of touch with the feelings and spiritual essence of the other person . . . as well as your own. Like nighttime slumber, this "ego sleep" is natural and normal and probably here to stay. It's best to make friends with it and forgive yourself in advance for drifting into it, since you'll be more likely to forgive others who drift into it while they're listening to *you*.

As you grow more secure in feeling your own spiritual essence, you'll probably doze off less into the grip of ego-centered listening. Give yourself plenty of loving acceptance for it, though, because we can tell you from much experience that criticizing yourself for these catnaps is no help at all in making you doze less. In fact, beating yourself up for slipping into ego-centered listening has about the same positive effect as a dog chasing its own tail.

As your ability grows in spirit-centered listening, you'll learn to love and accept yourself more and more. That's because the spirit holds everything in its embrace, including feelings, needs, old patterns, slipups, and recoveries. As your awareness of your spiritual essence grows, you'll be less tempted to grab on to an unpleasant emotion or an old pattern of defensiveness. It just won't feel as good to do it anymore—it will feel much better to

rest in the sweet spot of spirit, and from that place of spacious embrace to hold lightly all the comings and goings of your ego.

Ego Versus Spiritual

The word *ego* comes from Latin and simply means "I." When you think of yourself as "I" or "me," you're setting yourself apart from other people and the world around you. It's essential that you learn how to do this early on in life—if you can't distinguish yourself from walls and trees and cars, for example, your journey on Earth is likely to be harsh, calamitous, and brief. On the other hand, it's also essential that you learn to soften and melt the boundaries of your separate "I" so that you can enjoy the miracle of merging with loved ones and the world around you. If your ego rules the roost, you won't get free of it to enjoy the blessings of union; as a result, you'll miss out on much of the richness of life and love.

When your ego and spirit are in harmony with each other, the deeper magic of human existence comes to life. To feel a solid sense of "I-ness" while enjoying a deep, connected "us-ness" with your beloved is the essence of a spirit-centered relationship. And spirit-centered listening is a key practice in making this kind of relationship possible.

Spirit-Centered Listening Defined

Your spiritual center is the place that feels connected to yourself, to others, and to the universe as a whole. Imagine someone asking you, "How do you know that you're a spiritual being? How do you know that you're connected at the deepest level to others and the cosmos?"

You place your hand on your chest or belly and say, "Because I feel it *here*." Or perhaps you indicate an aura around your body with both of your hands and say, "Because I feel it *here*."

Where would you place *your* hand? Your spiritual center is where you personally feel your connection to the universe—it's not a concept or something you need to believe in. And in spirit-centered listening, you listen to others while feeling that center. As you become more aware of your own spiritual center, you'll experience a simultaneous growth of your ability to see and feel it in others.

The power of spirit-centered listening is such that it invites forth the spiritual center of others, even if they don't think they have one! As teachers and healers, we've seen this miracle occur so many times that we've developed an unshakable confidence in its power.

Ego-Centered Listening Defined

When any of us slips into ego-centered listening, we hear the other person through the filter of our own agenda, depending on what our egos want to hear. Common agendas are:

- Listening to find fault
- Listening to rebut
- Listening to be right
- Listening to fix

These are ego-centered filters that are based on the *listener's* personality, not on what the other person is actually saying. A typical example is when your partner tells you that he's tired. If you're listening through an ego filter (perhaps listening to find fault), you might instead hear this as, "I've been working a lot harder than you have." Based on this ego-filtered version of what your partner said, you might respond by saying, "You think *you're* tired! You don't know the half of what it feels like!"

Or if you're using the listening-to-fix filter, you might hear "I'm tired" as "I need you to tell me how to feel less tired." So from within the confines of your ego (in this case, your need to fix) you offer a solution: "Why don't you go to bed earlier instead of staying up 'til 11 reading spy novels?" Then you duck and feel unappreciated when several of those novels come flying past your head.

A certain amount of ego-centered listening isn't harmful to most relationships. Under stress, though, egos harden into defensive positions and symptoms escalate—your sense of "I" is essential, but under stress it can crystallize into "me, first and always." Then it becomes a hindrance to experiencing the love you want to feel.

When your ego is in charge to the exclusion of your spirit, you're usually focused on several goals:

- Getting approval
- Getting control
- Getting your needs met first

There's nothing wrong with any of these "get goals," just as long as you balance them with the corresponding "gives." If you're only focused on *getting* approval, for example, instead of *giving* equal amounts, the relationship will become lopsided. In fact, the common patterns most relationship therapists see are the direct result of imbalance caused by these ego-centered struggles:

- One partner is the thinker, and the other is the feeler
- One partner is the giver, and the other is the taker
- One person is the persecutor, and the other is the martyr

A bigger problem emerges if this lopsidedness is not addressed and balanced. More and more tension builds up over time—and under stress, the ego tends to lock into a defensive position that is driven by fear. Then our "get-goals" become more troublesome:

- Getting even
- Getting revenge
- Getting away
- Getting out

Listening from Your Spiritual Center

Let's shift gears here for a moment and imagine that your mate says, "You never bring me flowers anymore." If you slip into ego-centered listening, you'll immediately start to defend yourself. That's what we usually see people doing at first, before they experience the magic of spirit-centered listening. It's a very common way to respond, and it nearly always provokes a conflict.

When Partner A says, "You never bring me flowers anymore," in ego-centered listening, Partner B hears that statement as an attack. Partner B then gets defensive and demands, "What do you mean? Don't you remember that I brought you some roses on your birthday last year? I still have the receipt if you want to see it."

"That completely misses the point," says Partner A, with a heavy sigh.

And they're off and running around the well-worn track of a familiar argument.

If you're listening from your own spiritual center, however, you won't hear Partner A's statement as an attack. Instead, you'll hear deeper levels of what Partner A is actually saying.

You see, your spiritual center is always in a state of wonder and playful curiosity about who you really are and what you're becoming—as well as who others really are and what *they're* capable of becoming. The intention behind spirit-centered listening is to evoke the truth of what people are feeling while opening a new space of possibility for them to reach their goals.

In spirit-centered listening, you know that this conversation isn't really about the flowers, because you're able to hear the spirit of other people's communication instead of just the words.

So you hear Partner A saying, "I feel sad about what we've lost, and I want to reestablish a deep connection with you."

As you get skilled in spirit-centered listening, you'll begin to hear the feelings and the heartfelt intentions of other people more clearly. This doesn't mean that you have to overlook your own feelings and heartfelt intentions in favor of hearing others. As you'll see when you do the experiential process on the following pages, to practice spirit-centered listening is to be aware of your own feelings and inner experiences as you listen to your partner. In spirit-centered listening, you become presently aware of your own spiritual essence as you listen. From the open space of complete acceptance and deep connection you're offering, the person speaking to you opens a space of acceptance and connection in him- or herself.

Give yourself time to learn, though, and plenty of loving acceptance for being clumsy at it in the beginning. Even after practicing spirit-centered listening for 20-plus years, we still feel the pull of the ol' ego from time to time. Because we've practiced so much, though, we find that we don't get stuck in it for very long. It's important to keep in mind that when you're in touch with your spiritual center, you still have your ego, but your ego doesn't have *you*. That's because the feeling of spirit living within you provides a space or container for your ego and your emotions. You may feel scared or angry, but since you can sense those emotions occurring within the container of your spirit, you won't stay stuck in recycling the emotions for long.

Spirit-centered listening gets to the real issues quickly, because you don't have to fight your way down through layers of defensiveness and resistance. So our earlier dialogue might go like this:

Partner A: You don't bring me flowers anymore.

Partner B: You sound sad.

Partner A: I *am* sad.

Partner B: Part of me wants to defend myself and tell you that I brought you flowers for your birthday, but another part of me knows that's not the point. I hear you saying that you're missing something that used to be here in our relationship.

Partner A: Yes.

Spirit-centered listening opens a gateway of possibility for resolving issues like this—in fact, it paves the way and opens the space, and then illuminates each step along the way. At each juncture in resolving relationship issues, both partners are likely to feel the frequent pull toward ego-centered listening. With practice, though, you'll learn to notice this pull and slip free from the grip of the ego, spending more time communicating from your spiritual center. Real miracles become possible then, and although we've seen thousands of them unfold before our eyes, they always move and touch us.

Complete instructions for spirit-centered listening are given in Part II and on the CD that accompanies this book. We highly recommend that you take the time to go through these instructions carefully so that you can feel their full power at work.

Putting Spirit-Centered Listening to Work in Your Life

Daily life is full of opportunities to practice spirit-centered listening. The process works marvelously well in intimate relationships, of course, but its power can also be readily witnessed in relationships with children, friends, and co-workers. Every moment of relationship interaction is an invitation to tune in to the spiritual center of ourselves and those around us.

The closer we get to the very essence of ourselves and others, the more we realize that we're all exactly the same: We share the same yearning for connection, the same hunger for growth and change, and the same longing for transcendence. Spirit-centered listening is a practical tool for making your home in those magical realms of deeper communication.

❀ ❀ ❀ ❀

PART II

THE ESSENTIAL PRACTICES FOR GROWING A SPIRIT-CENTERED RELATIONSHIP

CHAPTER FOUR

COMPLETE INSTRUCTIONS

FOR PRESENCING SPIRIT

When you learn to rest your attention gently and lovingly on the sensations in yourself, you'll be richly rewarded by a wonderful surprise: the flowering of spiritual feelings. Around (and within) everything you feel will be the spacious sweetness of spirit moving in you.

This feeling comes forth naturally as a gift to you for learning to be present. It's been there all along, but until you sharpen your skills of perception through Presencing, you may not have noticed the background radiance of spirit. This fine, quiet hum moving in you is often drowned out by the noisier feelings of anger, fatigue, or anxiety—but if you learn to be present with those same feelings, you'll invariably notice that the subtle sensation of spirit is right among them . . . and as you become present to it, it will become much less subtle. What you pay attention to grows in your awareness, so the more you tune in to your spiritual essence, the more you'll feel its delicious pulsation.

Don't take our word for it, though—you can readily feel what we mean by a few minutes of personal experience. Treat yourself to a mindful, heartful journey through the experiential practice on the next few pages. (And for an even deeper experience, set aside some time to listen to the audio version of the practice, which is on the enclosed CD.) You'll soon see why we believe that Presencing spirit is one of the essential practices for illuminating the spiritual path of relationship.

Please note that we occasionally come across a person in our seminars who can get the full power of the following experiential practice in one "take," but most people need to go on several mindful journeys before being able to integrate the full significance of the instructions. Also, while some individuals can read and carry out the steps at the same time, most find that listening to someone else give them direction affords a much deeper experience. Feel free to experiment with both styles to find out which is best for you—that is, try reading the instructions yourself, then listen to the audio version or get a friend to take you through the steps.

The Purpose of the Presencing-Spirit Process

This chapter is designed to give you a personal experience of feeling your spiritual essence, which is always available if you know how to access it. You'll be focusing your awareness on more familiar feelings such as fatigue and anxiety. Then, by fine-tuning your awareness slightly, you'll learn how to tune in to the wonderful spirit that permeates even unpleasant things like fatigue or anger.

There is great value in learning how to feel your spiritual essence as an actual bodily experience, rather than as a concept. For one thing, it feels *good*—having free access to an all-natural pleasant sensation that you can have anytime you want is a great reward in itself! Even better, though, is the new relationship you'll be creating with the full range of your emotions.

Once you learn how to appreciate the bodily experience of your spiritual essence, you'll be much less likely to be overwhelmed or distracted by anger, fear, or other sensations. Note that until you can feel the spiritual essence that surrounds and permeates all of your emotions, you can sometimes be thrown off course by the emergence of anxiety, anger, or the like—but when you learn to feel spirit in the background, you'll begin to regard these emotions as natural occurrences on your journey rather than maddening distractions or path-altering disasters.

The ultimate gift of this process comes in your increased ability to feel the inner sweetness of spirit during the ups and downs and ebbs and flows of close relationships. All intimate partnerships go through pulsations of closeness and distance because we all come in to them with dual needs: the urge to merge and the urge to individuate. In other words, we all seek to lose ourselves in another person, while at the same time we all want true independence. The definition of a healthy relationship is the ability to be close to another person while simultaneously being completely yourself. The Presencing-spirit process is extremely useful in building the foundation for a relationship that gives you both unity *and* individuality.

The Instructions

Find a quiet place where you can work with this nine-step process without interruption for 20 minutes or so. We recommend doing it seated rather than lying down because there's less of a tendency to fall asleep if you're sitting upright. Also, the process is designed to help you in the "busy-ness" of daily life, so it's best if you don't think of it as something you have to lie down to do.

Step 1

Starting at the top of your head, be aware of your body's sensations without judging or trying to understand them. Use your awareness like a light and slowly scan down, all the way to your toes, being aware of any sensations as you go. Then do this several more times, taking at least ten seconds each time to scan your body from top to bottom.

When you're done, pause and consider your bodily sensations as a whole. First, notice if you feel any fatigue. There are no right or wrong answers to this inquiry . . . just see if you feel even the slightest amount of either. If you don't, move on to the next step; if you do, see if you can tune in to exactly what's telling you that you're tired. For example, if you feel thirst, there are specific sensations in your mouth that tell you so—but what exactly informs you that you're weary? For many of us it's a slight ache in the back of the arms and neck or a gritty heaviness in the eyelids—but be sure to notice what's letting you know that *you're* feeling this way.

Now get ready for a discovery that many people find life-changing: how to tune in to the natural spiritual feelings that are present even when you're fatigued. Rest your awareness again on the tired sensations in your arms and neck (or wherever you find them). Don't judge or analyze your tiredness . . . just be with it gently. As you focus on these sensations more intently, feel how in the center of them there is a sweet, clear, spaciousness— it's as if the tired sensations are the foreground and the open sensation is the background.

Now shift your awareness to feeling the outer edges of the tired sensations: Notice that the sweet spaciousness is all around the fatigue. As you grow more aware of this openness in and around the center of your tiredness, the clear feelings may come to the foreground, and your weariness may recede or even disappear. If you can sense that spacious openness clearly, just enjoy it. If you can't feel it yet, don't worry—there will be plenty of other opportunities to do so as we proceed.

Step 2

Now do your slow scan several more times, with a slight modification: As you go down from your head to your toes, rest your awareness mainly on the front of your body. Then when you get down to your feet, start to pay attention to the sensations on the back of your body, and slowly scan up along the back side of you. Think of it as a circle of awareness, going from top to bottom on the front of your body, then circling under your feet and going up the back.

Take at least ten seconds to sweep your awareness down the front of your body, and another ten seconds or so to sweep up the back. If you notice yourself judging or interpreting your body's sensations, just let go and return to simple, nonjudgmental awareness.

Step 3

Now fine-tune the process slightly, as you focus your circle of awareness primarily on your head and neck. Scan downward from the top of your head, being aware of the sensations on the front of your head, your forehead, your face, and your throat. Then circle around and scan upward from the back of your neck, the back of your head, and on up to the top. Finally, start your circle of awareness again, slowly moving down around the front of your head, face, and throat.

Do this several times, taking at least ten seconds to scan down the front, and ten seconds to scan up the back of your neck and head.

Step 4

Now let's do the same process with your torso: Begin your circle of awareness at your throat, and scan slowly down your chest, solar plexus, and stomach area to your lower abdomen; then circle around and scan slowly up your back. When you reach the top of your back where your neck begins, bring the circle around and begin again at the throat and go downward.

Do this several times, taking at least ten seconds to scan down through your chest and stomach, and at least ten seconds to scan up your back.

Step 5

Now we'll do the same process with your pelvis, hips, and legs. Begin your circle of awareness at your lower abdomen, and slowly scan down the front of your pelvis, your upper thighs, your shins, and down to your toes; then circle around under the soles of your feet and slowly bring your awareness up through your heels, your calves, the backs of your thighs, your hips, and your buttocks. When you get to the top of your buttocks, bring your circle of awareness over to the lower abdomen and proceed down again through the front of your pelvis. Do this several times, taking at least ten seconds to go downward and at least ten seconds to come up the back.

Step 6

Pause for a moment and appreciate yourself for what you've been doing. It's something we all probably could have benefited from learning in school. For most of us, though, our formal education doesn't include much training in the essential skills of living. Speaking personally, we both got six weeks of driver education in high school, but not even ten minutes' worth of training in how to notice our feelings, listen to another person, or solve a relationship problem.

Step 7

Getting back to the process, let's focus in on some of your specific emotions and sensations. By fine-tuning your sense of these familiar feelings, you'll be able to tune in to the more subtle spiritual awareness that this process is designed to facilitate.

There are three sets of sensations along the front of your throat, chest, and stomach that we'll be focusing on first, and then we'll look at another set in your upper back and neck. Each set has something very important to communicate to you, and is also a gateway to deeper spiritual awareness.

— Begin by scanning your **throat** and **upper chest.** Rest your awareness on this area for a few seconds: Do you feel any tight, heavy, constricted, or lump-in-the-throat sensations in this area, or does it feel open, free, and clear? There are no right-or-wrong answers here . . . just notice your sensations as you feel them. The constricted, heavy, lump-in-the-throat sensations are how most people describe sadness and longing, so notice if that's what you're feeling right now. Don't judge yourself or try to figure out *why* you might be feeling sadness or longing—just be right there with your sensations, resting your awareness on them gently and without judgment.

If you do sense any sadness or longing right now, let yourself feel these emotions deeply. As you do, notice that the clear, sweet sensation of openness is right there in the center of your sadness and longing. Feel the outer edges of these emotions, and be aware that the open, spacious sensations of spirit are all around that.

— Now scan another set of sensations located more in your **stomach area:** Do you feel any of the hallmarks of hunger, such as empty, gnawing pangs of contraction; or do you feel full and satisfied? Just try to detect whether you feel one or another of those sensations, doing your best to stay free of judging or interpreting them. (If you slip, just return to simple, nonjudgmental awareness as soon as possible.)

— Next, explore a third set of sensations located in the same general area as the hunger pangs you just tuned in to. Scan your stomach area, from your **solar plexus down to your navel,** and notice if you feel any of the butterfly sensations of anxiety or fear (some people also describe their anxiety or fear as "speedy" or "queasy"). Notice if you feel any speedy/queasy/butterfly sensations in your stomach area; or do you feel relaxed, calm, and at ease? There are no right or wrong answers—just be honest with yourself about what you pick up. Remember, all your emotions and sensations can be excellent gateways to the spiritual awareness that this process is designed to facilitate.

If you do sense hunger, fear, or anxiety, let yourself feel them deeply. Go right into the center of them with your nonjudgmental awareness. Keep tuning in until you can feel the open space and sweet clarity of your spiritual essence, right there in the center of your hunger or fear. Notice the area all around any sensations of hunger or fear, as well as where the outer edges of those feelings are. Determine how you can feel the sweet sensations of spirit all around hunger and fear, and down in the center of these sensations, too.

— Finally, focus in on the area **between your shoulder blades.** Scan up through your shoulders into the back of your neck and around into your jaw. Do this several times, being sure to sweep slowly. When you're finished, notice whether these areas feel tight, or are relaxed and pleasant. These are the areas that tense up when people are irritated or angry, so your muscles might be clenched if you're angry, and relaxed if you're not.

It's crucial that you don't try to interpret any of these sensations right now. This process is about learning to feel with greater awareness, not to make any judgments about it. If you feel any of the sensations of anger, rest your awareness right in the center of them. Notice as you do that the clear spaciousness of spirit is there, even in the midst of tension, anger, or any other sensations that you sense in your back, neck, and jaw.

Feel the outer edges of tension or anger, along with where those sensations leave off. Notice how you can feel the sweetness of spirit surrounding, and also down in the center of, those sensations.

Step 8

Now you're going to pick a set of sensations to focus on to fine-tune your awareness even more. This way, you'll learn to readily access your organic spiritual connection whenever you want to. So far you've focused on fatigue, sadness, hunger, anxiety, and anger; pick one that seems most interesting or compelling to you right now. For example, you might choose the one that has caused most concern in your relationships.

When you've selected what you'd like to focus on, rest your attention on those feelings and sensations. If you're focusing on fatigue, for instance, be aware of the achy feeling in the back of your arms or neck; if it's sadness, rest on the heaviness in your chest or the lump in your throat; if it's hunger, focus on the gnawing emptiness in your stomach; if it's anxiety, note the butterfly-speedy-queasy sensations in your stomach; and if it's anger, rest on the tight muscles between your shoulder blades or in your neck and jaws.

As you dwell on these sensations, take your awareness into the very center of them, feeling them as deeply as you can. And as you do, notice the sweet, clear openness that's in the center of them . . . even the most unpleasant ones. Keep resting your awareness deeper and deeper into the center of the sensations until you're clearly aware of a pleasant spaciousness. At the same time, spread out your awareness and notice that the clear, sweet openness is all around and behind the fatigue, anxiety, hunger, sadness, or anger, as well as in the center of it. Note, in fact, that the delicious sensation is in the background of everything else you're sensing—it's everywhere! It permeates your entire being.

Notice that wherever you rest your awareness, you can feel the spacious, clear sensation. This is your spiritual essence, or who you are at your deepest core level of identity. You may have heard the saying that you are a spiritual being having a human experience—well, this ever-present, all-over amazing sensation of spaciousness is the bodily feeling that lets you know how true that expression really is.

Learning to recognize the sweetness of spirit in the midst of your body's other sensations is like learning to recognize the sound of violins in a symphony orchestra: One moment you may not be able to pick them out from the other sounds, but once you do, you'll probably wonder how you overlooked them all along. This is understandable, though, because most of us haven't been taught to think of our spiritual essence as something we feel in our bodies.

Step 9

To conclude this exercise, let's anchor this feeling of sweet spaciousness so that you can come back to it whenever you wish. You can do so by repeatedly removing your focus from the sweet sensation and then returning to it—by doing so, you'll develop confidence in your ability to Presence spirit.

Put your attention on something far away from your body. Maybe rest your awareness on the wall farthest away from where you're sitting if you're indoors, or on a distant object if you're outdoors. Keep your attention on this faraway object for a moment, then return your awareness to your body, locating the spacious, pleasant sensation of spiritual essence within you. When you've securely located and felt it, take your attention away again and place it on the faraway object. Next, return your awareness to the spiritual essence deep within you, and feel its sweet clarity for a moment. Go back and forth a few times, casting your awareness far away and then returning home to the sweet feeling of spirit within you.

Now you're Presencing spirit by a simple act of your natural awareness, and from here on, it's just a matter of practice!

※ ※ ※ ※

CHAPTER FIVE

COMPLETE INSTRUCTIONS

FOR SPIRIT-CENTERED LISTENING

You're going to need a partner for the following process. If you're single, you can practice the 12 steps in this chapter with a friend, even if you're not romantically involved with one another. If you're part of a couple, you can practice with each other, of course, but we also recommend doing the process a few times with someone other than your mate. And if possible, have a third person read the instructions to both of you to keep you focused on moving through the steps as they're laid out.

(**Note:** It's important that both people do the Presencing-spirit process before learning spirit-centered listening, because the instructions below presume familiarity with the concepts and experiences taught in the last chapter.)

Step 1

Sit comfortably face-to-face, and take a few moments to get relaxed and ready to work.

The process begins with stating two simple commitments to each other, which open the gateway to learning and provide a structure in which the deepest transformation can take place. So when you're ready to begin, make eye contact and speak the first commitment to each other: "I commit to learning how to do spirit-centered listening with you, and to following all the instructions to the best of my ability."

Say your commitment to each other out loud, clearly and sincerely. When you finish, pause and relax for a moment. When you're ready, make eye contact and state the second commitment to each other: "I commit to discovering who I really am and what I can become, and to assisting you in discovering who you really are and what you can become."

When you're finished, take a few relaxed, deep breaths.

Now that you've set the stage by making these commitments to each other, get ready to learn something truly life-enhancing.

Step 2

This next step doesn't involve talking to each other—it's a silent process designed to help you get in touch with your spiritual center so that later, when you do talk and listen to each other, you'll be better able to stay connected on the spiritual level. Much of the magic of spirit-centered listening comes from what you do inside of yourself while you're in conversation with another person, so that's exactly where we'll begin.

Make relaxed eye contact with each other, then begin to scan your own body, beginning at the top of your head and moving down to your feet. Stay in eye contact with your partner while tuning in to your own body—as you do, you'll be learning how to be aware of your own feelings and sensations, while at the same time taking in what your partner is saying and doing.

Begin to create a "circular flow of awareness" between you and your partner: Tune in to yourself for a few seconds, then shift your awareness to the other person. Notice anything that catches your attention—the color of his or her eyes or the type of clothing he or she is wearing, for example. Then shift your awareness back to yourself. Focus on a feeling or sensation or any aspect of yourself, then go back to your partner. All you need to do for now is create a loop of awareness that flows back and forth from you to your partner every few seconds.

When you've established this flow of awareness, begin to circulate the following question back and forth: *Who am I at the deepest spiritual level?* Phrase the question silently in your mind, applying it first to yourself, then placing your awareness on your partner and applying the question to him or her. After you've shifted your awareness to your partner, wonder, *Who is this person at the deepest spiritual level?*

Even if you've known your partner for 30 years, you should act as if you've never even met him or her before. This state of fresh wonder creates a new opening each time for both of you to discover untapped depths in yourselves.

For a minute or so, let your awareness flow back and forth between you and your partner, pausing to ask the spiritual-level question of yourself and your partner. Just phrase the question silently and muse on it, keeping the circular flow of awareness going back and forth between you.

Now focus back on yourself and ask: *What can I become with full spiritual awareness?* When you feel ready, shift your awareness to your partner and silently phrase the question: *What can he/she become with full spiritual awareness?*

Let your awareness flow back and forth between you and your partner, pausing to ask the question silently in your mind each time. These questions are designed to open a space of wonder, not generate specific answers. It's okay for your mind to come up with answers, but don't dwell on them. Simply use the process to create a flow of wonder back and forth about who each of you really is and what you can become.

Step 3

Now focus in on something more specific: breathing. Create a circular flow of awareness in which you become aware of your own for a few breaths, then shift your attention to your partner. Tune in to the sights and sounds or his or her breathing—don't judge or analyze it. Just be with it for a few breaths, then circle your awareness over to your own respiration. After you've inhaled and exhaled a few times, loop your awareness over to your partner, tuning in to the rhythms of his or her breathing for several breaths.

Step 4

Now, instead of looping from yourself to your partner and back to yourself, be aware of your own breathing *at the same time* as you're aware of your partner's. You might feel your own chest rising and falling, while noticing the rising and falling of your partner's, too. You both should be within the same circle of awareness—not back and forth, but all one flow. Notice the differences between your breathing rhythm and your partner's. Perhaps one is faster, or another is deeper; neither one is right or wrong or better or worse . . . they're just different. All you need to do for now is be aware of your partner's breathing and your own at the same time.

Step 5

Now shift to being aware of sensations. Tune in for a few moments to your chest, becoming aware of what you're feeling there. Now shift your attention over to your partner, wondering about what he or she is feeling inside his or her chest. We can never really know what it's like inside another person, but we can always wonder and pay attention and be open to listening.

After you've spent a few moments wondering about the feelings inside your partner's chest, gently loop your awareness back over to your own. Go back and forth several more times between awareness of your own chest sensations and those of your partner.

Step 6

Now, be aware of your chest sensations while at the same time wondering about your partner's. Instead of shifting your awareness back and forth between you, be aware of both at the same time. Feel the inner sensations inside your chest as you simultaneously muse on those inside your partner's . . . both of you are inside a big circle of awareness.

Step 7

Now shift your awareness to the sensations in your abdomen. You might feel relaxed or anxious or hungry (or something else)—just focus on whatever you feel. At the same time, open your awareness to the sensations your partner might be feeling in that area. The important thing to learn in this part of the process is that you can be in touch with your own inner sensations and feelings while at the same time being aware of your partner's.

Step 8

Now direct your awareness to the sensations between your shoulder blades and up into the back of your neck. You might feel tense, relaxed, or in some pain (or something else), but just *be* with whatever you sense, using your nonjudgmental awareness. These areas in your upper back and neck get tense when you're angry or stressed out about events in your life, but just be aware of what you're feeling, not what it means. At the same time that you're scanning yourself, also include your partner's upper back and neck in your awareness. You probably won't be able to see that area, since your partner is facing you, but just notice that area. As you tune in to your own sensations in your upper back and neck, also wonder what your partner might be feeling.

Step 9

Now let's focus on feeling your own spiritual essence, as well as the spiritual connection between you and your partner. Notice the places in yourself where you feel that sweet, spacious sensation of spirit that's in and around all your other sensations. Stay in soft eye contact with your partner while you're taking note of the deliciousness of spirit within yourself. As you feel your own spiritual essence, be aware of your partner's, too, and wonder how he or she experiences it.

As you begin the speaking and listening part of the process in a moment, do your best to stay aware of your spiritual essence, as well as your partner's. When you lose awareness of it, do your best not to criticize yourself—just come back to your own spirit sensations, and also be aware of your partner's.

Step 10

Designate who will be Partner A and who will be Partner B. Both will have exactly the same opportunities to speak and listen, but Partner A will be talking first, while Partner B will listen.

Partner A will speak for two minutes about a significant, current relationship concern. Partner B must simply listen without offering any solutions, advice, or judgments. It's okay to use prompts such as, "Tell me more" and "Give me an example," but the listener should avoid any response that could be taken as positive or negative. If you're the listener, your main task is to *feel* your spiritual essence—and your partner's—while you listen.

After Partner A has spoken for two minutes, switch roles so that Partner B has a turn to speak for two minutes about a significant, current relationship concern.

When both of you have had your turns, pause and reflect on these questions:

- How much did you maintain awareness of your spiritual essence and that of your partner during the speaking and listening?

- Did you stay aware of it the whole time?

- Did you maintain it for a little while and then forget about it?

- Did you forget about it completely?

To spare you and your partner the trouble of criticizing yourselves for lapses in awareness, we'd like to tell you here that most people in our seminars completely forget about being aware of spiritual sensations when they start speaking and listening. That's why we call this a practice! It takes a lot of it to become proficient.

Now, before going into the next part of the practice, take a moment to tune back in to the spacious, sweet sensations of spiritual essence in you. Anchor your awareness in that essence, and then open your awareness further to include your partner's. Be aware of both of you as spiritual beings having a human experience. When you're in touch with the spiritual level in yourself and your partner, you'll be practicing the fully evolved skill of spirit-centered listening.

Step 11

In this step, you're going to focus in on the emotions underneath the words your partner is saying. You'll be taking turns speaking again, this time about a present relationship issue that concerns you. You can make it as deep or superficial as you wish, just as long as you're talking about something real.

Partner A will speak about his or her issue for two minutes. If you're Partner B, be sure to focus on tuning in to your spiritual essence and that of your partner. As you listen to the words your partner is saying, also tune in to the emotions beneath them. There are usually three such emotions that run along underneath words when people are speaking of real relationship issues—sadness, fear, and anger—so listen for those in the tone of Partner A's voice and in his or her body language.

When you're ready, make eye contact and begin with Partner A speaking for two minutes about a real relationship issue. Partner B, practice your spirit-centered listening as you also pay attention to the emotions under your partner's words. Keep the sweet, spacious sensations of your own spiritual essence in the background of your awareness as you listen to your partner.

After two minutes, switch roles so that Partner B has a turn to speak while Partner A practices spirit-centered listening.

When both of you have had your turns, pause to reflect on and discuss these questions:

- To what extent were you able to stay tuned in to your spiritual essence and that of your partner this time?

- Can you identify specific places where you lost awareness of the essence in you and your partner?

- If so, what were the triggers that lead to losing awareness? (For example, did you lose awareness when your partner started crying?)

Step 12

Finally, let go of the time constraints of the preceding practice sessions. Partner A will now speak about a significant, current relationship concern for as long as he or she likes, while Partner B practices spirit-centered listening—that is, without offering any solutions, advice, or judgments. It's okay to use prompts such as, "Tell me more" and "Give me an example," but the listener should avoid any response that could be taken as positive or negative. If you're the listener, your main task is to *feel* the spiritual essence of both yourself and your partner while you're listening.

When Partner A is finished speaking, switch roles so that Partner B gets a turn. Continue until you reach an organic stopping place.

❀ ❀ ❀ ❀

PART III

SPIRIT-CENTERED SOLUTIONS
TO RECURRING
RELATIONSHIP CONCERNS

CHAPTER SIX

A Spirit-Centered Way for Singles

to Manifest a New Relationship Partner

Many single people (we also include divorced individuals in this group) have come to work with us during the past three decades, and by far the most frequently asked question is: "How can I create a healthy new relationship in my life?" The unspoken plea under this concern is, "I want to stop making the same mistakes over and over again with the partners I choose."

In helping people attract new love into their lives, we've found that a spiritual principle, if correctly understood, works quickly and effectively to address this concern, so in this chapter, we'd like to share it with you. We first learned it ourselves "the hard way" by struggling through many difficult relationships in our 20s and early 30s. Once we understood the following principle, however, we met each other and began the union of our dreams. And now we offer this powerful tool in the hopes that it will work its magic in *your* life.

The Key Concept

If you align your natural resources correctly inside yourself, you'll effortlessly attract the life experiences that would best serve you. If the forces are *not* aligned correctly, however, you're going to overcompensate by shifting into the stressful pursuit of trying hard to bring those experiences to you. Unfortunately, the act of stressful pursuit actually has the opposite effect of what you intend: It repels the very situations you're trying hardest to attain.

In attempting to manifest a new mate, many single people waste time and energy doing more of what already hasn't worked. They place more and more emphasis on the outer world, even as they neglect to make the inner shifts that would bring a new relationship to them with no strain whatsoever.

So what can *you* do to correctly align the forces inside yourself?

The major barrier that stands in the way of establishing a truly intimate relationship with another person is an unloved part of yourself. A hidden aspect of you—that is, something you've never fully accepted—is preventing you from bringing genuine love into your life. Even if you could bring a healthy new relationship into your life, this unloved part of yourself will rush forward to prevent you from enjoying and keeping it. In other words, the unloved part of yourself acts as a repellent to keep a healthy relationship at bay until you've learned to generate your own unconditional self-love.

If you don't love yourself, you'll always be looking for someone else to do it for you . . . and this never works. You see, people who don't love themselves attract other people who don't love themselves—and then they try to get others to care for them unconditionally, when all the while they're not even doing it for themselves. But when you love yourself deeply for everything you are (and aren't), you'll attract people who love and accept themselves the same way.

If you don't love a part of yourself, you're going to run around in desperation trying to get someone else to love you. Subconsciously, your hope is that if another person gives you enough love, that part will go away. It never does—only a moment of loving yourself unconditionally will do that particular job. If you finally stop running from that unloved part of yourself and confront it, you'll see that it's generally just one of the following:

— **The fear of abandonment.** You can probably see why this could wreak havoc on your relationships. (It certainly did in our early relationships, before we became aware that it was driving a lot of our troublesome behavior.) When you're afraid of being left alone, you'll either keep people distant so that it won't hurt so much if they leave you, or you'll cling to them dependently so that they can't leave without dragging you with them.

— **The fear of being smothered by another person.** When you're in the grip of this one, you're worried that your individuality and freedom will be lost if you surrender to full union with the other person. So you stay at arm's length, just as a person who's afraid of drowning might stand a yard or so away from the water's edge.

The important thing to know about any fear, including the ones above, is that it's simply a pulsating quiver of racy-queasy sensations in your stomach area. Fear, said the legendary psychiatrist Fritz Perls, is merely excitement without the breath. So breathe into what's frightening you and watch what happens: The butterflies will flutter out of hiding and fly away. In other words, deep, easy breathing dispels fear.

In addition, when you love your fears directly, you can actually feel them disappear. And where they used to be, you'll now notice a big open space into which a wonderful new relationship can enter. That's what happened to us, and that's what we've seen happen to countless people when they mustered the courage to love themselves *and* all their fears.

How to Break the Grip of Fear

It's impossible to enjoy a good relationship until you give that scary place in yourself just a split second of love. You see, fear gets stirred up when you let people in too close, so to keep it under control, you keep others at a distance—yet, in the process, you're pushing down the very aspects of yourself that most need to come to the surface and be loved. Then, having already judged yourself as unlovable, you strain to get others to love you. But trying to do this is on par with a dog chasing its own tail: The more anybody tries to love you, the faster you run from them.

Fortunately, you can solve that problem right here by asking yourself what you're feeling right now. Tune in to yourself and do a quick body scan: Are you afraid that the ideas in this book may not work for you—or that *nothing* will work? Are you worried that maybe you're not good enough to do this practice? Do you fear, as we once did, that there's something fundamentally wrong with you that's always going to keep you from love? Whatever it is, feel all your feelings and *love* them right now. And love yourself for having them—and your courage to experience them.

We've never met anyone who loved themselves deeply and unconditionally all the time, so don't expect that you'll be perfect at it either. Begin with just a second or two of loving yourself and work up from there. But first, *start* with a commitment to love yourself—that way, you'll have it to fall back on when you find yourself in the grip of your unlovable part.

Remember, too, that loving yourself has nothing to do with egotism or self-flattery. Egotistical people are desperately trying to get other people to love them, even as they feel deeply undeserving inside. That's why egotism and boasting look so tacky: Everybody knows it's phony.

What we're talking about here is genuine, sincere, heartfelt, and humble love for yourself. It's a feeling of accepting yourself for everything you are *and* aren't. Unless you're superhuman, you won't ever feel absolute love and acceptance for yourself all the time—but you *can* make a commitment to feeling that way. Making a commitment to loving yourself gives you firm ground to stand on throughout the ups and downs of your life . . . in your relationships and beyond.

✿ ✿ ✿ ✿

CHAPTER SEVEN

ENDING JEALOUSY

AND CONTROL STRUGGLES

You may have encountered the piece of spiritual wisdom found in *A Course in Miracles* and other sources that says that nothing real can be threatened, while nothing unreal exists. To that end, the reason people have trouble eliminating jealousy from themselves and their relationships is because jealousy isn't real—so trying to eliminate it is like trying to grab soap bubbles.

Remember that famous quote from Albert Einstein that says it's not possible to solve a problem in the same state of consciousness in which it was created. In helping thousands of people, we've never seen that statement be more true than in the elimination of jealousy from relationships.

Jealousy Is Really about Fear and Control

The only way to handle the issue of jealousy is to shift your state of consciousness so that you can see it for what it really is. The dictionary tells us that jealousy is when you're "fearful of losing affection or being supplanted by another person." It also says that we're jealous when we're "vigilant in guarding something." These are helpful pointers to understanding the real issues underneath such a powerful emotion.

When you're jealous, you're scared. There is no question that the *fear* is real—you can feel the reality of its racy-queasy-butterflies in your belly when you notice that you're afraid of losing your partner's love. But you can make fear worse by expressing it in the distorted form of anger. In other words, if you could tell your partner, "I'm scared that I'm losing your love," you'd move through the mire of the situation much more quickly. Yet instead of confronting your fears directly, your pattern is probably to get angry and blame your partner—and this keeps you from focusing inward to find out what you're *really* scared about.

When you're jealous, you're also trying to control the other person and his/her feelings—and this is where many people have gotten into very sticky relationship dramas. One of us (Gay) recalls the painful experience of getting dumped at 19 by a girlfriend:

I'd been in love with Alice since we were seniors in high school. I think from the moment I met her, I assumed we'd always be together. Then, in our sophomore year of college, she fell in love with another guy. I went through many levels of anger before I was finally able to confront my real fears and grief. First, I angrily tried to talk her out of it by listing all the faults and flaws of the guy she was dumping me for. I made up lies about him and hurled them at her, and I detailed why I was infinitely superior to him. When none of that worked, I tried guilt: How could she betray everything we'd gone through together? Yet nothing I tried worked. In fact, the harder I tried to hang on to her, the more I saw the love in her eyes turn to pity.

You see, the reason control never works is because whether or not another person loves you is completely *out of* your control. Two thousand years ago, Epictetus made this point clearly in the opening line of his manual on conscious living, *Enchiridion:* "The secret of happiness becomes yours when you realize that some things are within your control and some things are not." The reason jealousy is making you so miserable is because you're expending your energy trying to control another person, rather than turning that energy inward to explore your real feelings.

Getting Free of Jealousy Is a Two-Step Process

First, it's imperative that you find out what you're really afraid of. The fears of abandonment, of being alone, or of not feeling whole and sufficient on your own are what's behind jealousy; however, you probably have your own particular "signature" of feelings, so you need to turn your attention deeply enough inside to discover, "What fear is my jealousy really based on?"

There's often grief as well as fear buried beneath the jealousy. You've probably never fully recovered from some earlier abandonment or betrayal, for instance, and the open wound of this old trauma is what's driving your desperate attempt to control the other person in your present. Just as with fear, we each have our own signature of grief, so the only way to discover it is to open up to yourself in an attitude of genuine innocence and wonder by asking, "What old hurts are beneath my feelings of jealousy?"

The second step is to resonate with the fears that you discover. It's also good to talk about your feelings openly, preferably with the person you're jealous of; however, talking doesn't tend to do much good unless you've let yourself fully feel the fear inside.

This is where resonance really helps. This principle says that the best way to "get rid" of something is to not try to get rid of it at all. Instead, simply be with it, resonate with it, and feel it thoroughly. Then talking about it can be helpful, because your words are coming from deep contact with the fear.

The problem with talking issues out is that words can often be used to avoid contacting the actual experience of the fear, so take time to resonate with the issue first, and then communicate with the key person. A friend, coach, or therapist may also step in to provide the support and listening ear we all need at such times.

What's Possible

In a healthy, conscious relationship, jealousy doesn't recycle because the partners talk about it on the deeper level we've described here. They discuss their fears, their old griefs, and what they want and need from the other person in the present.

Keep in mind that if you get underneath the anger and control of jealousy to the real feelings of fear and grief, you'll find that the negative emotion dissolves naturally and doesn't return.

❀ ❀ ❀ ❀

CHAPTER EIGHT

REKINDLING SEXUAL PASSION

In working with many couples, as well as in the personal experience we've gained from our own marriage, we've found that absolute honesty is crucial to a long-lasting, vibrant, and harmonious relationship. You've heard the cliché that honesty is the best policy, but what may surprise you is hearing that it's also the best aphrodisiac there is. And because total candor brings peace of mind along with it, it's also the best way to get a good night's sleep afterward.

Honesty is such a powerful sexual stimulant because if there is any significant truth you haven't communicated to your partner, you're going to crimp the flow of comfortable communication between you. And when the flow is shut down, you not only forfeit the right to expect a good relationship with your partner, but you also experience a reduction in sexual desire.

Any significant withheld truth stops the flow of harmony cold, and sexual energy is quick to follow. Most people don't realize this simple principle, so when things aren't going well in their relationship, they think that the other person is the source of what's wrong. We've found, though, that it's wise to look on one's own front doorstep first. If you don't feel sexually turned on to your partner, or if you're having trouble getting a good night's sleep, you've probably withheld some truth that needs communicating.

Here are some of the most popular examples of such truths, drawn from the couples we've worked with:

- I've had sexual experiences I haven't told you about.
- I've spent money you don't know about.
- I've got _____ and haven't told you about it.
- I'm still angry about _____.
- I'm still hurt about _____.
- I'm scared about _____.
- I really want _____,
  and I'm afraid to tell you.

It's important to note that *any* withheld truth can crimp the flow of sexual desire in a relationship—not just ones that involve sex in some way. Most people tell us that they haven't been honest with their partner because "he/she really doesn't want to hear the truth" or because "I don't want to hurt her/him." When our clients get under these superficial excuses, the reason usually turns out to be: "I haven't told the truth because I don't want to face the consequences." And under that lies the real reason: "I haven't told the truth because I fear living at the highest level of creativity and energy, and lying is one way I've learned that will reliably dampen my energy."

The Positive Side

People dread telling the truth because they fear the consequences, but in actual fact, we've only seen *positive* consequences for being honest in the long run. We've seen hundreds of relationships come to life again after the revelation of some significant truth. Yes, there's often a short-term flurry of upset following the explanation, but the ultimate outcome is usually a more stable and higher-functioning relationship. The surprising payoff is that sexual desire comes to life again in the wake of the truth telling.

Now, how do you actually do this? If you want to rekindle sexual passion by revealing some withheld truths, you'll likely have better success if you follow a few simple guidelines drawn from real-life experiences with hundreds of couples:

— First, get agreement from your partner that he or she wants a transparently honest relationship. This is done by asking a few simple questions. Look your partner in the eyes and say something like this: "I'd like a completely honest relationship with you, where nothing is ever hidden. Would you like to have a completely honest relationship with me, or would you rather I keep things to myself if I think they might upset you?"

Most people choose the honesty option. If your partner does so, this is your signal that he or she is willing to hear the truth. If your partner says no, then save it for another time.

— Once you're in agreement that you both want honesty, deliver the significant truth in as few words as possible. Don't justify it, embellish it, or explain it. Just lay it out, pure and simple, as in, "I've been having an affair," or "I don't want to visit your parents this Christmas." That's the easy part.

— Now you have to give your partner room to express his or her reaction fully. There will likely be anger, sadness, threats, or retribution—and your willingness to let these reactions emerge determines whether the resolution will be quick or slow. If you get defensive and put on the brakes, you'll be delaying the positive payoff that is yours at the end of the day.

From bearing witness to hundreds of such sessions, we can tell you that there is indeed a positive payoff to all of this: When the truth is out and the noise of reaction has subsided, a new flow of harmony and vibrant energy springs to life. And this new energy is the raw material of physical passion. We've received hundreds of reports from happy couples whose sexual relationship began to flourish anew immediately after the revealing of a significant truth.

❀ ❀ ❀ ❀

CHAPTER NINE

How to Know When to Leave

a Troubled Relationship

In the process of giving talks and seminars on relationships for three decades (and accumulating a million-plus frequent-flyer miles along the way!), we've been asked literally thousands of questions from audience members. Two of the most common are: "How do I know when to leave a troubled relationship?" and "How do I make sure that I don't repeat the same mistakes in a new relationship?"

Often troubled unions consist of one partner who takes too much responsibility for it and one who takes too little. The partner who takes too much responsibility tends to feel guilty about whether he or she has done enough, while the other is usually quite accomplished in feeding that guilt by constantly claiming the victim position.

If *you're* someone who takes too much responsibility for how your relationships go, you need to be on the lookout for signs that you've gone too far, which include guilt, worry, fatigue, and the erosion of your health. Your task is to take 100 percent responsibility—but don't stray over into 110, 150, or 200 percent. A relationship between two people comprises 200 percent responsibility, which must be divided absolutely equally into each person taking 100 percent.

We make a point of mentioning the issue of responsibility because individuals who ask the kinds of questions on the previous page are invariably those who take far too much of it. Their big trap is thinking that everything is their fault, which keeps them from requiring their partners to take equal responsibility. They often stew in indecision about whether to leave or stay . . . and continue to do so for months or years until they've eroded their self-esteem, their health, and their creative energy.

To know whether to leave is a personal decision, and it requires a certain type of deeply personal awareness to find the answer. We use a somatic, spirit-centered approach to helping people discover their own answers. To use our technique takes the commitment to ask two questions and the courage to accept the honesty of the answers you receive from your body and spirit.

The First Question

We ask people to consider this question first: "Does the pain you feel about the relationship overshadow its possibilities?"

To better illustrate how to use this question, check out the following bit of dialogue, taken from a lecture where a woman named Helga asked us how to know whether she should leave her relationship.

Us: Begin right where you are now. Scan your body and your feelings, using your nonjudgmental awareness. Don't evaluate how you feel inside . . . just be aware of all your feelings.

Helga: Okay.

Us: Can you feel the pain of the relationship? The sum total of all the anger and sadness and despair about it?

Helga: *[pauses for ten seconds or so]* Yes.

Us: Where do you feel it mostly?

Helga: My chest. And my back.

Us: Okay. Let yourself accept all those feelings . . . just be with them nonjudgmentally.

Helga: All right.

Us: And remember how in the early days of the relationship you felt possibility and hope and excitement?

Helga: Yes, of course.

Us: Look inside yourself now and find out if the pain has completely overshadowed the possibility. Is there possibility left?

Helga: *[pauses for 30 seconds or so]* No, I can't feel it. I can't remember feeling that in a long time.

The Second Question

Us: Now please consider one more question.

Helga: Okay.

Us: Can you live with the consequences of leaving right now: where to live, reactions of family, all those consequences?

Helga: *[beginning to cry]* Yes, I believe so. I think I have to. I've talked to my children about it, and I think they understand.

Us: Okay. You don't have to decide permanently right this second, but hopefully this process has helped you clarify where you are. Now before we finish, please take a moment to scan your feelings again, and this time notice if you can feel some open, spacious feelings that are behind and around all those painful feelings like anger and sadness. Your spiritual essence—the person you are deep inside—isn't really affected by all those painful feelings. It doesn't ever go anywhere, but sometimes we lose touch with it because the painful feelings are so compelling.

Can you feel the sweet spaciousness of your spirit in the background of all your other feelings?

Helga: *[smiling slightly]* Yes. Yes, I can feel that. It's been a while since I felt it.

Us: But you feel it now, and that's what's important. Take a moment to appreciate it, and to appreciate yourself for your courage.

No Right or Wrong Answers

There are never any right or wrong answers to the big questions of life. Likewise, such questions can only be answered from within. That's why we invite the person to tune in deeply to discern their own solutions. When people raise their hands at a lecture to ask us whether it's time to leave a trouble relationship, we believe that they're asking for (and deserve) something much larger: a tool for finding the answers to their most profound questions.

❀ ❀ ❀ ❀

CONCLUSION

GOING FORWARD

This book's journey of learning will soon conclude, but for you and us—and all those fortunate enough to feel the beckoning of spirit-centered relationship—the journey continues to infinity. One of the great blessings of relationships is that they provide endless opportunities for growth and enlightenment. If you commit to using all of your partnership interactions as learning moments, you'll be guaranteed a rich and exhilarating ride through life. Speaking personally, we've never had a boring moment in our many decades of marriage and working with the relationships of others.

We hope that the concepts and tools in this book have brought a fresh, new wave of passion to all your moments of life and love. If our paths cross in person, and we hope they do, we'd be delighted to hear about your adventures in the wild territories of love.

For now, go with our blessings to do your sacred work of creating a spirit-centered relationship. Thank you for hearing the call and for granting us the gift of your precious attention.

❁ ❁ ❁ ❁

ABOUT THE AUTHORS

Gay and **Kathlyn Hendricks** have worked together throughout the three decades of their marriage. They are the co-authors of nine books together, including such bestsellers as *Conscious Loving* and *The Conscious Heart.* Their work has taken them to more than 30 countries around the world and onto more than 500 television and radio programs. They have two adult children and two granddaughters, and make their home in Ojai, California. They may be contacted through their Website: **www.hendricks.com**.

❀ ❀ ❀ ❀

HAY HOUSE TITLES OF RELATED INTEREST

The Love Book, by John Randolph Price

Love Notes: 101 Lessons from the Heart,
by Jim Brickman and Cindy Pearlman

Mars Venus Cards, by John Gray

101 Ways to Romance, by Barbara De Angelis, Ph.D.

*A Relationship for a Lifetime: Everything You
Need to Know to Create a Love That Lasts,*
by Kelly E. Johnson, M.D.

*Secrets of Attraction: The Universal Laws of Love,
Sex, and Romance,* by Sandra Anne Taylor

❀ ❀ ❀

All of the above are available at your local bookstore,
or may be ordered through Hay House
(see the page after next).

❀ ❀ ❀